AF438621

Introduction

Are you fed up with the way your food tastes? You can't find fresh, healthy food in supermarkets. Or, the food from the farmer's markets spoils too fast for you to eat. Although additives and artificial colors can cause health problems, there are no other options in modern food supply. Perhaps you've recently discovered a passion for hunting, fishing, and gardening but don't know how to preserve it. This book is for you!

You will learn how to preserve healthy food with modern food safety techniques using "Canning for Beginners - How to Preserve Quality Food, Make Money and Build Self Reliance".

This is not something you can do in your grandmother's kitchen. These instructions will help you eliminate all the hassle of canning, freezing or dehydrating food. We can help you prepare delicious home-preserved foods, whether you are starting with fruits, vegetables, and meats. Each step is broken down into steps to guide you through the preservation process.

Each method is carefully evaluated and listed with all the drawbacks and benefits. This will allow you to choose the best method for your needs. Which method is best for you: freezing, canning, or dehydrating? Consider the supplies that you will need to do each and determine how much you can afford for this new hobby. Check to see if equipment that you were given by your great aunt is still in use. We can give you the definitive information you need about what you need and in what condition to ensure your success.

We can help you spot problems and give tips to fix them.

These simple recipes will help you get started with the wonderful adventure of making your own preserves. If you have an apple tree in your backyard, preserve it! Start preserving if you or a friend discover a wonderful strawberry farm just down the street. Start preserving if your hunting or fishing trip was a success! This book is the best place to begin!

Why Canning?

Since the beginning of time, humans have tried to preserve food. All over the globe, drying, salting, or fermenting food is still practiced. Canning is an addition to the growing list of ways we can preserve food. Napoleon Bonaparte offered a reward to anyone who could find a way to preserve food safely and efficiently. Nicholas Appert, 15 years later, introduced the first heat-processing method for food, sealing it in clean jars and waxing them. As science improved, much more has been done to improve the process over the next 100 years.

We are now in the 21st century. Canning is a great hobby. First, food preservation is still important. Our food supply is more reliable, diverse, and abundant than it was 50 years ago. However, commercial preservation is still necessary.

There have been many questions about the health effects of these commercial methods. Cans of commercially canned food often have higher levels of sugar and salt than homecanned foods. Some manufacturers add other ingredients to enhance the flavor, texture or nutrition of foods. You can preserve your food's healthful benefits by canning at home.

Second, canning is a great way to live a greener lifestyle. You can preserve fresh fruits and veggies that you grow yourself, or that have been grown close to you, without having to travel thousands of kilometers. This reduces the carbon footprint of food processed in commercial kitchens.

Home canning is an excellent choice for food preservation because you can guarantee the freshest food. You can guarantee high-quality, fresh food when you buy local produce or grow it yourself. You can ensure that your produce is fresher than canned food by canning it at home.

The last, but not least, is the pure satisfaction that comes with opening a canner of summer produce and being able say, "I canned it!"

How Canning Works

Fresh foods lose their freshness, which can be caused by oxygen loss, moisture loss, activity of food enzymes and microorganism growth. Fresh foods naturally contain oxygen, moisture, enzymes, and other elements. These elements start to degrade as food ages and lose their freshness. As fresh food ages, microorganisms like yeast, bacteria, and mold grow quickly and can get into food via insect damage, bruises, or diseased food tissue.

Safe home canning techniques remove oxygen and destroy enzymes. They also prevent the growth and spread of bacteria, mold and yeast. Properly canned jars have a vacuum seal that keeps liquid in place and air out.

Equipment Needed

You will need some basic equipment to start canning. These basic pieces may seem appealing to you, so before you accept their offer from your older relatives or friends, make sure they are in good working order. They can be purchased at any store that sells basic canning supplies if they are not in good condition.

1. Canners

A water bath canner, a large kettle with a rack that allows you to submerge filled jars in boiling water, is called a water bath. This is a good method for making preserves, jams and pickles, as well as preserves, jams and tomatoes. These foods are more acidic so they can be cooked at the boiling point of the water (212 F or 100 C). The kettle should be deep enough to cover the jars with water. It should also have a rack to keep the jars in place and a tight fitting lid.

A pressure canner can be used to can low-acid foods. To be safe for consumption, meats, fish, poultry, as well as vegetables that have a low acid content must be cooked at temperatures between 240-250 F (115-121 C). Only a pressure canner can achieve this at home. These canners include a jar rack, a gasket, safety release, and steam vent. When pressure canning, it is important that you strictly follow all instructions.

2. Jars

There are many sizes and shapes of canning jars, but they all come in tempered glass and are specifically made for canning. Half-pints and pints are the most popular sizes. Avoid using jars made from pre-prepared foods as they can break or leak during home canning. Canning jars must be free from chips and cracks. Jar rims should also be smooth for a good seal.

3. Lids

Flat metal lids for canning jars are the most popular. They have a sealing compound ring on the underside and a screw top band that holds it in place. Flat lids should only be used once. However, screw top bands can be reused if not bent or rusted.

A second type of lid is made from zinc and has a porcelain lining inside. This lid must be used in conjunction with a rubber sealing band. These lids are less popular than the two-piece ones. These rubber rings should not be re-used, and the porcelain in the zinc cap shouldn't have cracks or chips.

4. Other useful equipment

Other than canners and lids, canners and jars can also be used to make canning easier and more secure. As a canning kit, you will find a wide-mouthed funnel, jar lifting tool, and a non-metal utensil to release air bubbles from filled containers. The vegetable brush is a good tool to clean your vegetables. For canning, sharp knives and a food processor or food mill are required. A large kettle, Dutch oven, or other cooking tools are also useful.

Steps in the Canning Process

You should choose foods that are freshest when canning foods. You should can them as soon as they are picked. The fruit should be firm but not brittle and free from bruises. Vegetables must be tender and young, with no bruises or blemishes. Home slaughter of meat and poultry is recommended. Once cool, you should can them as soon as you can. You should never allow meat or poultry to be taken from sick or diseased animals. After harvesting seafood and fish, it is important to immediately ice them and then clean and canner within two days.

To ensure even cooking, thoroughly clean all food and cut it into equal pieces.

There are two methods to pack food for canning. Cold-packing involves placing uncooked food in sterilized containers and then pour boiling liquid over it. The liquid could be water, juice, syrup, or a combination of both. Foods with high starch content like corn, peas and lima beans should not be packed loosely when cold-packing. These foods expand because they absorb more liquid during canning.

Hot-pack canning is a method that involves partially cooking the food and then packing it loosely in sterilized jars.

The cold-pack and hot pack methods share some basic steps.

1. For flaws, check lids and jars. Rinse with hot soapy water and then rinse in cold water. Finally, heat the water in a pot of water for 10 minutes to sterilize. The kettle can be taken off the heat. However, you should leave the lids and jars in the boiling water until you are ready for them to be filled.
2. Only prepare enough food to canner one. You should work as fast as possible to ensure that the jars are hot. You can either clean the food and cut it before you start to prepare the lids and jars. Or you can do this while the lids and jars are being cleaned. Make sure to follow any recipe.
3. Hot jars are best for food. Make sure you leave enough headspace. The amount of space between the top and liquid in a jar and the rim is

called headspace. This allows for expansion of the food and liquid during processing. The correct amount of headspace can affect whether or not the lid seals correctly.

4. Make sure you add the boiling liquid to the saucepan, ensuring that there is enough headspace.

5. To release any air bubbles, gently slide a non-metal object around the jar. If necessary, add more boiling liquid.

6. Use a moist, clean cloth or paper towel to wipe the rim of your jar. A perfect seal can be prevented by small pieces of food or liquids.

7. Add the lids. Flat lids: Place the sealing compound around the jar's rim and screw the band on tightly to secure it. Wet the rubber ring and place it over the mouth of your jar. Attach the zinc cap to the rubber band by screwing it down. Turn it around 1/4 inch or 1/2 cm. Screw the zinc cap securely to seal the seam after the process is complete.

8. According to the recipe directions, fill the jars with the right canner. After placing the jars in the canner, ensure that they are fully covered with boiling water. Before you start the processing, place the lid on the canner. Place the filled jars in a pressure canner. Make sure they don't touch. The canner should be covered and locked. Turn the heat on high. Adjust the heat to allow steam to flow at a moderate rate. Allow the steam to flow for 10 minutes at a steady speed in order to exhaust any air trapped within the canner. Turn on the pressure and close the vent. For more information, always refer to the manufacturer's instructions. Keep the heat on high until the canner gauge registers 10-15 pounds pressure. Follow the instructions in the recipe. Always allow the pressure canner to cool down before removing the jars. Follow the instructions on how to open the canner.

9. Place jars on rack to cool. Allow air to circulate between the jars, placing them slightly apart.

10. After the jars have cooled completely, seal them. Flat-topped lids won't give when you press down on their center. If this is the case, you can remove the screws bands. If the lid bounces around, it is possible that air may enter the jar. You can either repackage and process the entire time in another jar with a different lid or refrigerate it and eat it

within.It will keep for a few days. You can also use other types of lids to seal the jar if the lid is upside down.

Once you have completed the canning process label the jars with your date, food and batch number, if there were multiple batches. You can keep them in a dark, cool place for up to one year.

Food Safety for Canning

Before you can taste or use canned vegetables, meats and fish at home (except tomatoes), it is very important to boil them for between 10-20 minutes. For the entire 20 minutes, boil corn and spinach. To avoid scorching, you can add water. These foods can harbour bacteria, even if they are canned at home. Cooking will kill the bacteria. These foods should not be eaten straight from the jar. You should immediately throw out any food that appears to be leaking or has a foamy, cloudy, or off-smelling liquid.

If the lid isn't leaking, you can place the container in a bag and seal it. If the seal is damaged or leaky, you should treat it as toxic and follow these steps before disposing of it.

<u>Detoxification Steps:</u>
1. Use disposable rubber gloves or heavy plastic gloves to place the contaminated jar into a large kettle.
2. Use soap and water to wash your hands. Take the gloves out.
3. Cover the jar with water. Be careful not to get the water out of the kettle. You should fill the jar with water for at least 1 inch.
4. Cover the kettle with a lid, and bring water to boil.
5. Boil the food for at least 30 seconds to ensure that the components of the jar have been detoxified.
6. Cool the jar. Discard all food and the lid.

7. All surfaces and items that have come in contact with the contaminated jar should be cleaned and sanitized.Freezing Foods

You can also freeze food to preserve it. This process has some advantages and disadvantages.

The main advantages of freezing are that it requires less equipment and is easier than canning. However, the main drawback is that cold temperatures don't destroy microorganisms or enzymes as heat canning does. Instead, they slow down their growth and activity. Certain foods lose their texture when frozen, thawed or cooked. Frozen foods can't be stored as long as canned food. If power is unavailable to freeze food, frozen food can be at risk.

You probably have the equipment you need to freeze in your kitchen. Plastic freezer bags in various sizes, plastic wraps or rigid plastic containers with sealed lids are all good options for freezing food. Containers should have tight fitting lids. Use freezer tape to seal food wrap.

A large kettle and a basket to blanch foods are also essential equipment. This involves boiling fresh foods for a short time and cooling them in ice water. This prevents enzymes from working and preserves the nutrients and color of vegetables. A timer is also important.

Steps to Freezing Foods

1. Pick top-quality, fresh, and ripe vegetables or fruits that are free from bruises or blemishes. You can freeze them immediately after they are picked or buy them as soon as possible.
2. Use cold water to wash fruits and vegetables and then prepare them according the specific recipes. Sort or cut into uniform pieces.

3. After blanching the food as needed, place it in containers. Leave enough headspace. This allows liquid and food to expand as it freezes. It also helps prevent freezer burn and cracking.

4. Use a damp cloth or paper towel to clean the seal and seal it. Rigid plastic containers should have tight fitting lids that you can seal and then "burp", to remove any air. You can "burp" the lid by pressing down and lifting the edge of it in one spot. Then, seal the lid again. The plastic bags should be tightly fitted around your food with as little air possible. Follow the manufacturer's instructions and zip or seal the bag using a twist tie, freezer tape or other methods.

5. Be sure to label the containers with the contents, the amount and the date.

6. You can freeze small quantities at 0 F (-17 C). You should leave enough space between the packages. Place them on plates or freezer coils to let the cold air circulate and allow the food to freeze as fast as possible.Frozen foods can be kept at the same temperature up to one year depending on what type of food they are.

Fruits and Vegetables: Store for 8-12 Months

Poultry - Shop for 6-9 Months

Fish - Keep for 3-6 Months

Ground meat - Keep it in the fridge for between 3 and 4 months

You can store cubed or processed meat for up to 1-2 months

Food Safety for Freezing Foods

It is crucial to be able to identify what to do in the event that your freezer stops working. Keep your freezer closed if it stops working. Food inside the freezer will likely stay frozen for approximately two days.

You can also move food from one freezer to another if your freezer stops working. To prolong the safety and health of frozen food, you can pack it in ice.

You can only refreeze frozen food that has reached a temperature of 40 F (4.5 C):

1. If ice crystals remain in vegetables, they will not show any signs ofspoilage.
2. Fruits are free from signs of spoilage.
3. If ice crystals remain, shellfish and cooked food can be used.
4. If they are free from mold growth, breads, nuts and baked goods will be safe.If the freezer temperature is higher than 40 F, you should immediately throw away all meats, poultry and creamed foods!

Cooking it right away is another way to save food that has been partially thawed (upto 40 F). You can refrigerate food that is not ready to eat immediately if it isn't possible to eat right away.

Dehydrating food

One of the oldest methods of conserving food is drying it. Drying foods has the advantage that they shrink and can be stored in larger quantities. The downside is that drying can affect the nutritional value, taste, and appearance of food. The foods remain closer to their original flavor, appearance, and nutrition by freezing and canning. Canning and freezing takes longer than either canning, or freezing.

To dry food, dehydrating involves heat, low humidity, and circulation. You can use the oven, the sun or a commercial dehydrating device. You will also need racks or baking sheets to place your food on and a sharp knife to cut larger items.

Foods at their peak freshness should be used for dehydrating. Once the food is prepared, it must be cleaned, cut into uniform pieces and placed on racks that allow air to circulate around them.

After the food has been dried to your specifications, you can store it in a dry, clean container for up to one year. Dehydrated foods last twice as long in cool, dark storage than fruits. Meat jerky can be stored at room temperature for up to 2 weeks, 3 to 6 months in the fridge, and up 1 year in the freezer.

Ways to Dehydrate Food

Sun Drying

Fruit is the only food you can safely dehydrate in the sun. Fruits are safe because of their high sugar and acid levels. This reduces the chance of them spoiling. It is necessary to have heat levels above 85 F (29 C) for 3-4 days, and humidity below 60%. If possible, a steady breeze should be provided. It is especially difficult to dry food in the sun in the South because of these conditions. California is the ideal climate for drying fruit. They have made a business out of drying grapes and raisins!

Pretreat your fruit with an acidic solution such as citric acid, ascorbic acid or lemon juice. This will help speed up the drying process and prevent light fruits from getting too dark in storage. These solutions can also kill potentially harmful bacteria. These products can be found in most supermarkets. After soaking the fruit for approximately 10 minutes or according to the package directions, drain the fruit on absorbent towels.

Fruits with hard skins or waxy coatings should be cracked or checked before drying. These fruits include grapes, cherries and figs. For 30-60 seconds, place the fruit in briskly boiling water. Use absorbent towels to drain the fruit.

Clean fruits and fruit slices should be placed on a safe screen or rack. Many screens purchased in hardware stores are galvanized with zinc or cadmium, which can cause food to oxidize and leave harmful residues. Avoid screens made of aluminum or copper, as these can damage the vitamins and discolor the food. Place the rack or screen on top of a sheet of aluminum or zinc to get the maximum sun energy. To discourage birds and insects, cover the fruit with a second screen or cheesecloth. You should bring the fruit racks inside every evening as cooler temperatures can cause condensation to build up on the screens. This will slow down the drying process.

Pasteurize your sun dried fruit to kill any insects or eggs that may have been present during drying. You can pasteurize sun-dried fruit using one of these methods:

<u>Oven method - Place fruits in one layer on a tray, or shallow pan. For 30 minutes, bake in an oven preheated at 160 F (71 C). Cool, then seal as directed.</u>

<u>Freezer Method: Place fruit in an airtight container. Freeze at 0 F (-17 C), for 48 hours. Repackage fruit for storage.</u>

Oven Dehydrating Food

The household oven appropriate for dehydrating food must have a setting for 140 $\frac{238}{92}$ F (60 $\frac{238}{92}$ C). Any higher temperature will cook the food instead of drying it. Convection ovens are the best, since they have a fan built into the oven. Otherwise, you may need to keep the oven door ajar and have a fan running to circulate the air adequately. This makes an oven impractical for drying large amounts of food.

For using your oven to dehydrate, follow the same recommendations for fruits as listed in Sun Drying Fruit.

Vegetables should be clean and cut into uniform pieces or slices per recipe recommendations. Blanch the pieces in boiling water, and chill only until you can touch them and place them on an absorbent towel. Place on racks that fit in a cookie sheet, leaving space around each piece for air circulation.

Meat recipes usually involve placing meat in a brine or marinade for a time. Follow such recipes exactly and use the utmost care to keep your work surfaces clean. Place the treated strips of meat on a rack that fits in a cookie sheet, and allow for air circulation.

Drying foods in the oven can take many hours. Check the food periodically, and test for doneness.

Commercial Dehydrators

A commercial food dehydrator is a small household appliance that can more quickly dehydrate foods. It has an electric element, and a fan to circulate air within the appliance. The advantage is that this can be done more quickly and efficiently than in the sun or your oven. The disadvantage is that they may hold much smaller batches of food.

You will find commercial dehydrators of various sizes, quality, and price at many department stores, kitchen stores, or online. Follow the manufacturer's instructions for processing on your specific appliance. <u>How to Tell if Your Food is Dehydrated</u>

Regardless of what type of dehydrating you utilize, you can judge if your food is dry by the following guidelines.

1. Fruit should be dehydrated until it has about 20% moisture left. Cool atest piece, then cut it in half. No moisture should be evident, even

when squeezed. Some fruits may remain pliable, but should not be sticky to the touch. Berries should move freely when placed in a small container together.

2. Vegetables should only have about 10% moisture left when they aredehydrated.   This will leave them crisp, or brittle. Some will even shatter when hit with a hammer.

3. Meat should be tested after the first 3 hours. Cool a piece slightly, andbend it gently. It should crack, but not break when dehydrated. Once food is sufficiently dried, cool and package in dry containers.

Food Safety for Dehydrated Food

If condensation develops in dried foods, spoilage can develop. Check on dried foods periodically during storage for signs of condensation and spoilage. Particularly with fruits, you may want to check on the packages for the first time 7-10 days after storage. If you see signs of too much moisture, such as condensation, remove the food from package and dehydrate again. If there are signs of spoilage, such as soft spots and mold, discard the food.

Dried fruit may be eaten as dehydrated, or reconstituted. Dehydrated vegetables should be reconstituted before consumption. Meat jerky is generally eaten as dehydrated.

To reconstitute food, soak in water until desired volume and texture has returned. Dehydrated vegetables can be places as is in soups and stews. They will reconstitute as the soup boils.

If your reconstituting food is in water for more than 2 hours, refrigerate the food for the remaining time required.

Recipes for all methods

Before you begin, here are a few tips to ensure your success in most recipes.

1. Times written in canning recipes are written for canning at sea level. Ifthe processing for water bath canning is 20 minutes or less, add 1

minute for each 1000 feet above sea level. Add 2 minutes for each 1000 feet above sea level if the processing time is more than 20 minutes.

2. You will also have to adjust the pressure specified in the recipes forpressure canning in higher altitudes. For spring-dial gauges, increase the pressure by 1 pound for each 2000 feet above sea level. For instance, if the recipe specifies 10 pounds of pressure, and your elevation is 2000 feet, increase the pressure to 11 pounds. If your elevation is 4000 feet, increase the pressure to 12 pounds. For weight gauges, follow the manufacturer's instructions for adjusting pressure for higher altitudes.

3. Fruits that will be canned are packed in syrup. Combine the sugar andwater as listed below and heat in a saucepan until the sugar dissolves. After heating, skim foam off the top as necessary. Plan on using 1-1 1/2 cups syrup per quart of fruit, or 1/3-1/2 cup per pint. Quantities listed here produce the different syrups you may choose:

Type of Syrup	Cups of Sugar	Cups of Water	Yield (cups)
Very Thin	1	4	4 ¾
Thin	2	4	5
Medium	3	4	5 ½
Heavy	4 ¾	4	6 ½
Very Heavy	7	4	7 ¾

4. You can use the same syrup for freezing fruit, or you can pack with orwithout added sugar, or water. Make sure to leave enough headspace for expansion.

<u>Preserved Apples</u>

2 ½ - 3 pounds ripe, firm apples for each quart

Ascorbic acid color keeper prepared according to package instructions *or*

2 Tbsp. Salt, 2 Tbsp. Lemon Juice, and 1 gallon water

Rinse, peel, core and slice apples into uniform slices. Dip apples into ascorbic acid or lemon juice mixture. Drain well.

Water-Bath Canning (Hot –Pack): In a kettle, prepare desired syrup according to chart above. Prepare 1-1 ½ cups syrup for each quart of apples. Boil syrup; reduce heat. Add prepared apples to syrup and return to boiling. Remove from heat. Using a slotted spoon, fill hot, clean jars with apple slices, leaving ½ inch headspace. Return syrup to boiling. Pour enough boiling syrup over apples to cover, leaving ½ inch headspace. Wipe rims, adjust lids, and process in a boiling water bath for 20 minutes. Start time when water boils.

Freezing: For an unsweetened pack, mix ½ teaspoon ascorbic acid color keeper into each 4 cups of cold water. Allow 1 – 1 ½ cups water for each quart. Pack apples into moisture-vapor proof freezer containers, leaving ½ 1 inch headspace. Add enough of the water to cover apples, still allowing for headspace. Seal, label, and freeze.

For a sugar pack, dissolve ¼ teaspoon ascorbic acid color keeper in ¼ cup cold water. In a large bowl, place 4 cups of apples, and then sprinkle ascorbic acid mixture and ½ cup sugar. Stir to mix. Pack apples tightly into freezer containers, leaving headspace. Seal, label and freeze.

Dehydrating: Place treated apple slices in a single layer on trays, pit side up. Dry in the sun, the oven, or a commercial dehydrator until soft, leather, and pliable. There should be no moist area in the center when cut in two.

<u>Strawberry Jam (Water Bath Canning)</u>

8 cups fresh, firm strawberries, stems removed

1 1 ¾-ounce package powdered fruit pectin

2 Tbsp. Lemon juice

7 cups sugar

In a large bowl, crush strawberries down to measure 4 ½ cups. Combine crushed berries, pectin, and lemon juice in an 8-10 quart kettle. Bring to a full rolling boil, which cannot be stirred down. Stir in sugar. Return to a full rolling boil. Boil hard, uncovered, for 1 minute, stirring constantly. Remove from heat and quickly skim off foam with a metal spoon. Ladle at once into hot, clean half-pint jars, leaving ¼ inch headspace. Wipe rims; adjust lids. Place jars in rack and process in a boiling water bath for 15 minutes (start timing when water boils). Remove from canner and place jars upside down on a clean towel for 30 minutes so the fruit does not float to the top of the jar. Flip right side up and cool. Makes 7-8 half-pints.

<u>Preserved Tomatoes</u>

2 ½ - 3 pounds ripe, firm tomatoes per quart

Salt

Wash tomatoes thoroughly and remove stems. Drain. Put tomatoes into a wire-mesh basket and dip into boiling water in a large kettle for 30 seconds. Remove from boiling water and place immediately into cold water. Slip off skins and discard. Remove cores and stem ends. Small or medium tomatoes may be preserved whole, but cut large tomatoes into quarters or eighths. For dehydrating, they can also be sliced.

Water-Bath Canning (Cold-Pack): Pack tomatoes tightly into hot, clean jars, leaving a ½ inch headspace. Using a wooden spoon, press tomatoes gently until some of their juice runs out. Add more tomatoes and press gently to fill spaces. For quarts, add 1 teaspoon salt. For pints, add ½ teaspoon salt. Do not add water. Wipe jar rims; adjust lids. Process in a boiling water bath; quarts for 45 minutes, pints for 35 minutes. Start time when the water boils.

(Hot-Pack): Prepare tomatoes, leaving whole or cutting into halves. Bring tomatoes to a boil in a large kettle, stirring gently. Boil, uncovered, for 5 minutes. Pack hot tomatoes and some of their juice into clean, hot jars, leaving ½ inch headspace. Add salt as listed above. Wipe jar rims; adjust lids. Process in a boiling water bath as listed above.

Freezing: In a large kettle, bring tomatoes slowly to boiling, stirring constantly. Cover and simmer gently for 10 minutes, or until tender. Set kettle into ice water to cool. Package into freezer containers, leaving ½ -1 inch headspace. Add salt, 1 teaspoon for quarts, or ½ teaspoon for pints. Seal, label, and freeze.

Dehydrating: Prepare tomatoes as above. Blanch for 1 minute in boiling water. Slice or cut tomatoes into ¾ inch sections. Small pear or plum tomatoes should be cut in half. Place on lightly oiled racks or trays of oven or commercial dehydrator, leaving space between pieces for air circulation.

Place in oven preheated to 140 $\frac{238}{92}$ F (60 $\frac{238}{92}$ C), or   follow instructions for your commercial dehydrator. Dry until leathery, but not tacky. Cool, seal in a dry container, label, and store.

<u>Preserved Beans (Green or Wax)</u>

1 ½ to 2 ½ pounds fresh, young green or wax beans for each quart

Salt

Wash beans, draining well.   Remove ends and strings. Leave whole, or cut into 1-2 inch pieces. For French style, slice diagonally end-to-end.

Pressure Canning (Cold-Pack): Pack as tightly as possible without crushing in clean, hot jars, leaving ½ inch headspace. For quarts, add ½ tsp. Salt; for pints, add ¼ tsp. Salt. Pour boiling water over beans, leaving ½ inch headspace. Wipe jar rims; adjust lids. Place in racks and process in a pressure canner at 10 pounds pressure. For quarts, process 25 minutes; for pints, process 20 minutes. At 15 pounds pressure, process 15 minutes for either quarts or pints.

(Hot-Pack): In a large kettle, bring enough water to cover beans to boiling. Add beans and cook 5 minutes on high heat. Remove from heat. Pack hot beans loosely into hot, clean jars, leaving ½ inch headspace. Add ½ tsp. Salt for quarts, or ¼ tsp. Salt for pint jars. Pour in boiling cooking liquid, leaving ½ inch headspace. Wipe rims; adjust lids. Process at the same pressure and for the same amount of time as listed above for cold-pack pressure canning.

Make sure that you boil canned beans at least 10 minutes before tasting. Add water if needed.

Freezing: After preparing beans as above, place in a blanching basket. Submerge 1 pound beans in 1 gallon boiling water in a large kettle. Cover and blanch for 3 minutes. Begin timing immediately after submerging beans. Remove basket, and plunge beans into ice water. Cool for 3 minutes. Drain well. Package into moisture-vapor proof containers. Shake down to pack beans closely, leaving ½ inch headspace. Seal, label, and freeze. Dehydrating: After preparing beans as above, blanch for 2 minutes. Drain and cool slightly. Place on lightly oiled rack for commercial dehydrator or oven, leaving room between pieces for air circulation. Place in oven preheated to 140 $\frac{238}{92}$ F (60 $\frac{238}{92}$ C), or   follow instructions for your commercial dehydrator. Dry until crisp. Cool, package, label, and store.

<u>Preserved Meat</u>

This recipe can be used for beef, veal, lamb, pork, or venison.

2 pounds meat per quart, freshly slaughtered

Salt

Boiling water or meat stock

Chill meat immediately after slaughter, or purchase meat fresh from a reliable butcher and refrigerate and can as soon after purchase as possible. Trim fat, gristle, and bones from chilled meat, and cut into pieces that will pack easily into canning jars. For freezing, cut into desired sizes and portions. Make sure to keep your work area and utensils very clean.

Pressure Canning (Hot Pack): Slowly cook meat to medium done in a small amount of water or meat stock in a pan covered with a tight lid. Stir occasionally and season lightly with salt. Drain. Pack the hot cooked meat loosely into hot, clean jars, leaving 1-inch headspace. Pour in boiling water or meat stock to cover the meat, again leaving 1-inch headspace. Wipe jar rims, and adjust lids. Process quart jars in pressure cooker at 10 pounds pressure for 90 minutes, pint jars for 75 minutes.

When cooled, check for proper seal, label, and store. Make sure to boil canned meats in a small amount of water for at least 15-20 minutes before tasting or using!

Freezing: Separate individual portions with two layers of waxed paper. Seal in plastic freezer bags, or wrap in butcher paper, taping with freezer tape. Label and freeze.

Dehydrating: (Meat Jerky) After meat is chilled, partially freeze to make it easier to slice thinly. Meat for dehydrating should be no thicker than ¼ inch. Trim all fat from each strip. If chewy jerky is desired, slice with the grain of the meat. If more tender, brittle jerky is preferred, slice across the grain of the meat. Utilize a meat tenderizer according to package directions, if desired. Meat may be marinated for flavor and tenderness in a mixture of ¼ cup soy sauce, 1 Tbsp. Worcestershire sauce, ¼ tsp. Black pepper, ¼ tsp. Garlic powder, ½ tsp. Onion powder, and 1 tsp. Hickory smoke flavored salt. Place 1 ½ - 2 pounds of lean meat strips in a shallow pan and cover with marinade. Cover and refrigerate 1-2 hours, or overnight. Bring strips of meat and marinade to a boil and boil for 5 minutes. Drain and dry meat strips. Place meat strips on rack for dehydrator or to place in an oven. Make sure they have space between for air circulation. Place in a commercial dehydrator and follow manufacturers' instructions. If using an oven, preheat oven to 140 $^{238}_{92}$ F (60 $^{238}_{92}$ C) Begin checking samples after 3 hours. Meat strips should crack, but not break when bent. Pat off excess beads of oils with absorbent toweling when done, and cool. <u>Preserved Poultry</u>

This recipe will work for chicken, duck, turkey, or game birds that have been freshly slaughtered.

3 ½ to 4 ¼ pounds poultry for each quart canned with bone, or 5 ½ to 6 ¼ pounds per quart without bone

Salt

Boiling water or Broth

Rinse chilled, dressed poultry in cold water. Pat dry with a clean cloth. Cut up, removing visible fat. Boil, steam, or bake until medium done. The pink color of the meat should be almost gone. Remove the bone, if desired, but don't remove the skin.

Pressure Canning (Hot-Pack): Pack poultry pieces loosely into hot, clean jars. Place drumsticks and thighs with skin next to glass, and fit breast pieces into the center, leaving 1-inch headspace. If desired, add 1 tsp. Salt to quart jars, or ½ tsp. Salt to pint jars. Cover poultry with boiling water or broth, leaving 1-inch headspace. Wipe rims; adjust lids. Place in rack and process in pressure canner at 10 pounds pressure. For poultry with bones, process quarts for 75 minutes and pints for 65 minutes. For de-boned poultry, process quarts for 90 minutes, and pints for 75 minutes. Cool, label, and store. Make sure to boil canned poultry in a small amount of water for 15-20 minutes before you taste or use it in a recipe!

Freezing: Disjoint and cut up poultry, or leave whole. Wrap in moisturevapor proof wrapping. Wrap and freeze giblets separately. Seal, label, and freeze.